This Journal Belongs to..

....

....

AF429780

Year Of Interview

....

All about My DAD

Name of My DAD:

His Mother Name:

His Father Name:

His Profession:

Currently we are living at:

....

....

....

....

I'm going to ask some questions to my DAD about his life, I hope that, it'll be enjoyable moments. 1...2...3... let's start...

DAD! You are welcome in an interview with me on you, let's introduce yourself first...

DAD! What's your Date of Birth? Why your year of birth is remarkable?

Tell me about the family members of you when you were a child...

What can you remember about your Grandparents? Tell me some sweet memories with them you had....

Who was your best friend & why he/she was best?

____

____

____

____

____

____

____

____

____

What can you remember about your elementary school?

____

____

____

____

____

____

____

____

Who was your best Teacher in whole educational life and why?

How did you manage your parents when they became angry with your stupid work?

Tell me something that was really special to you at your university/collage life....

What differences you find between your generation and present generation?

Tell me one of your bad habits your mom didn't like?

____

____

____

____

____

____

____

____

Did you have nick name & what was that? Who gave you that name?

____

____

____

____

____

____

____

____

____

Tell me a memory of your child age you will never forget......

What was most important advice of your Dad for you?

Who was your best childhood cousin and why he/she was best?

What foods did you liked most at early age? Do you still like to have these?

____

____

____

____

____

____

____

____

____

Tell me the names of some books you have read and I should read those also....

____

____

____

____

____

____

____

____

Which family weeding you'll never forget and why?

Now tell me some hobbies of you and why you think that these are important for us?

What was the hardest thing you overcome as a child and how did you handle it?

What are your favorite movies and why these are your favorite?

Who was a great coach of your life? What specialty makes him/her great?

Whom do you feel most who is no more...? Why he/she was important to you?

What's your feeling when you visit a graveyard?

Do you like pet? Which one is your favorite?

When did you have married? When you saw mom for first time and where?

Tell me about yours wedding party....!

What was your feelings being father for first time? What special things you did at that time?

What do you teach your children about money?

What did your father teach you about life?

What was the most embracing moments of your life? What happened there?

What are the similarities between you and your father?

What are the similarities between you and your Mother?

What did your mother teach you about life?

What did your mother teach you about life?

What were 3 best virtues of your Mother?

Which food was most delicious cooked by your mother?

What was the special gift you ever received?

____

____

____

____

____

____

____

____

Which holiday do you like most? Why?

____

____

____

____

____

____

____

What was your first job? How old were you when you started working? What was your feeling when you got your first salary?

What are your advices to be successful in life?

What are the key points to select someone as a good friend?

Which sports do you like? Have you played it? When did you play it last time?

____

____

____

____

____

____

____

____

Who are your favorite players? Why do you like them?

____

____

____

____

____

____

____

____

Do you enjoy your family life?

What do you expect from your family?

What are the key points you think to be a successful father?

Does mom really like you? What do you think about it?

Which activities of my mom you really dislike?

Do you feel proud of your Wife? Why?

What else you expect from your wife?

What are the special things you have done to surprise your wife?

What are the key factors to choose a life partner? What do you think about this?

What are your suggestions to your children about love and relationship?

____

____

____

____

____

____

____

____

____

____

____

____

Did you propose any girl before mom? Who it was?

____

____

____

____

____

____

Remember a fault you did but you shouldn't that?

What are your favorite quotes?

What are the adjectives your grandparents used to call you?

What are the memories of your grandpa you still miss?

Mention some places you have already visited and some places you want to visit? Among them which one do you like best?

What is your retirement plan?

Which political party do you support and why it's for?

What is the name of your favorite person? Why do you like him/her?

Name three habits in you that people don't like?

What was most unexpected thing happened to you?

Are you an extrovert or introvert?

Do you think religion is import for our life? Why?

What's your opinion about others religions?

What is your favorite flower?

What is your favorite Smell?

What is your favorite animal?

What is your favorite outfit?

What is your favorite curry?

What are your favorite fruits?

What's angers you and how do you handle it?

Give a short definition of life from your own point of view

Which issues make you to feel sorrow?

What brings you joy?

Do you believe in supernatural power? What's your logic in-this regards?

If you became a super hero what's things you'll do first and why?

Ten advices to your children to do/not to do.....

If you became a president (lol) what's things you'll do first and why?

If you win prize money worth $10000000, what will you do with that?

If you found me and mum stuck in danger, whom will you save first? (lol you are in confusion)

____

____

____

____

____

____

____

Give a proof that you love me.....

____

____

____

____

____

____

____

____

____

____

Which TV Programs do you enjoy now and why?

Who is your favorite Television Actor/Actress?

Which Television program was your favorite at childhood? Do you still miss it?

Which one was your favorite cartoon character?

When did you cried loud for last time? What reason it was?

Do you believe in Luck? What's logic behind your believe?

What's was your life plan? Is it going as you planned?

Did you steal food from kitchen when you were a child?

Did you face punishment from your parents? What it was and why?

What was the best day of your school life you remember?

What did you do when you need to poof at class time?

____

____

____

____

____

____

Have you ever slap anyone?(if yes) Why?

____

____

____

____

____

____

____

____

____

____

____

What was the first place you stayed away from home? What was the purpose?

Tell me about your best Aunt! Do you still miss her?

How often you visited your Nana's House? Tell details about them.

Who is your favorite Uncle and why he is different from others?
Tell me some memories of you with him.

What were the stupid things you did at your teenage?

Who taught you to drive? How long it was taken to pass?

Do you know how to swim? (If yes) Who taught you how to swim?

Where did you first swim?

Did you ever get jealous of someone? (If yes) Why?

What were the three happiest moments of your life?

What are the similarities between you and me?

What you expect from me?

The Last one is not a question it's a request...
Ten Wishes for me....

1.

2.

3.

4.

5.

6.

7.

8.

9.

10.

_______________________   _______________________
Signature of Interviewer   *Signature of DAD*

DAD thanks a lot for your patients and times you gave to me. I hope that you have enjoyed these questioning. I have learned a lot of unknown topics about you. Hope that it'll help me to shape my life. If you found any mistake during this interview I am sorry for that. Good Wishes & love for your Dad.

The End